C000092089

Written in a clear and captivati[...]
us on a journey in search of the s[...]
the game truly beautiful. Drawi[...]
religion, he presents deep truths about life and faith through the
use of football allegories. His explanations are simple yet profound,
uplifting yet challenging. He also shares some of the highs and lows
of his own life, ranging from his wedding to a newspaper's chosen
'Bride of the Year' to the tragic loss of a close friend at Hillsborough.
Chester's warmth, honesty, humility and good humour shine
through this book, which is a truly captivating blend of wisdom
and homely anecdotes. I recommend it highly.
PETER LUPSON, AUTHOR, *THANK GOD FOR FOOTBALL!*, SPCK, 2010

Football offers us great enjoyment, whether to school kids playing in
a park with jumpers as goal posts or to crowds watching a vital game
in one of our mega stadia. Winning seems to bring most happiness,
but for those who look deeper, football offers more: a chance to
contribute to a team; an opportunity to improve on one's best, to win
by playing the right way, to be tested by the challenge the opposition
provides; and the possibility of learning lessons in the present for
use in the future. This book gets beyond the surface of football, and
reminds us that we need to get beyond the surface of life, too.
REVD JOHN K. BOYERS, CHAPLAIN, MANCHESTER UNITED

Text copyright © Mark Chester 2015
The author asserts the moral right
to be identified as the author of this work

Published by
The Bible Reading Fellowship
15 The Chambers, Vineyard
Abingdon OX14 3FE
United Kingdom
Tel: +44 (0)1865 319700
Email: enquiries@brf.org.uk
Website: www.brf.org.uk
BRF is a Registered Charity

ISBN 978 1 84101 654 2
First published 2015
10 9 8 7 6 5 4 3 2 1 0
All rights reserved

Acknowledgements
Page 15: 'You'll Never Walk Alone', copyright © 1945 by Richard Rodgers & Oscar
Hammerstein II. Copyright Renewed. International Copyright Secured. All Rights
Reserved. Used by Permission of Williamson Music, A Division of Rodgers &
Hammerstein: An Imagem Company.

Unless otherwise stated, scripture quotations are taken from The Holy Bible, New
International Version® (Anglicised edition) copyright © 1973, 1978, 1984, 2011 by
www.biblica.com, Biblica, Inc.® Used by permission of Hodder & Stoughton Publishers,
an Hachette UK company. All rights reserved. 'NIV' is a registered trade mark of
Biblica. UK trademark number 1448790.

Scripture quotations taken from The Holy Bible, New International Version, copyright
© 1973, 1978, 1984, 1995 by International Bible Society, are used by permission of
Hodder & Stoughton, a member of the Hachette Livre UK Group. All rights reserved.
'NIV' is a registered trademark of International Bible Society. UK trademark number
1448790.

Scripture quotations from the Contemporary English Version of the Bible, published by
HarperCollins Publishers, copyright © 1991, 1992, 1995 American Bible Society.

Cover image © Per Magnus Persson/Johnér Images/Corbis

Every effort has been made to trace and contact copyright owners for material used
in this resource. We apologise for any inadvertent omissions or errors, and would ask
those concerned to contact us so that full acknowledgement can be made in the future.

A catalogue record for this book is available from the British Library

Printed and bound by CPI Group (UK) Ltd, Croydon CR0 4YY

THE SOUL
OF FOOTBALL

One man's story of football, family and faith

Mark Chester

In memory of John McBrien (1971–89)

Contents

✤

Preface

The origin of football

Once upon a time an architect decided to begin work on a new project. His design was original and innovative, and eventually it led to a blueprint for a sport that would obsess the world. This is how it all began.

God created the first ball:
In the beginning God created the heavens and the earth.
GENESIS 1:1

God set aside a piece of land:
And God said, 'Let the water under the sky be gathered to one place, and let dry ground appear.' And it was so.
GENESIS 1:9

God grew some grass:
Then God said, 'Let the land produce vegetation: seed-bearing plants and trees on the land that bear fruit with seed in it, according to their various kinds.' And it was so.
GENESIS 1:11

God turned on the floodlights:
And God said, 'Let there be lights in the vault of the sky to separate the day from the night, and let them serve as

signs to mark sacred times, and days and years, and let them be lights in the vault of the sky to give light on the earth.' And it was so.

GENESIS 1:14–15

God made players:
So God created mankind in his own image,
  in the image of God he created them;
  male and female he created them.

GENESIS 1:27

We humans then got involved. We made some rules, picked the teams, decided on a time to kick off—and the game of football was born!

❖

Foreword

Occasionally when you meet someone for the first time, you just know you are going to get on well with that person. This was my experience when I first met Mark Chester about five years ago. This positive feeling was not because I met Mark at Anfield, although it helped, as I am a big Liverpool fan. Neither was it because Mark insisted on driving me back to the train station after the meeting because of the rain, although obviously such kindness helps in friendship. It was something deeper; it was that sense of meeting a kindred spirit.

In reading his book, it makes sense why I connected so easily with Mark and why he is the person I like to 'hang out' with when our paths cross at conferences. Mark speaks my language, the language of football, with more than a hint of humorous insight and slightly mischievous banter. If you know football, then when Mark talks or writes about it, you can feel, visualise, hear, smell and almost taste the game. Mark understands the power of football as well, especially when it is integrated within a story.

While recognising the power of football, Mark is not naïve; he understands its limitations and longs for something deeper, beyond the game itself. This is where my connection with Mark really flourishes, as we see the impact of football through the lens of primary relationships with friends, family and, even more profoundly, with God.

For both of us football is a microcosm of life. What you experience in football you can experience in life—joy, sadness, pain, victory, disappointment, elation. Thus from the experience of football you have the possibility to teach and educate about life. This is what Mark does, using the game in order to enhance precious relationships. Therefore Mark stands on the shoulders of early church writers such as the apostle Paul in taking the well-known reality of sport in order to impart spiritual truth.

The application of Mark's experiential learning approach I have grown most to appreciate is in the father–child relationship. For over 20 years in my work with the Christian charity Ambassadors Football, we have tried to deal with consequences of broken father–child relationships: gang membership, addiction, marginalisation, vulnerability, misplaced sense of identity, low self-esteem, criminal behaviour, alienation. In the last few years we have stumbled across a potential upstream solution to these problems, which is to invest in and support the father–child relationship and mobilise positive father figures for the next generation of children and youth. The solution we stumbled across at Ambassadors, Mark discovered years ago, hence we draw on Mark's insight and experience to strengthen through football the crucial relationship between a dad and his kids.

Mark speaks my language, he understands the 'beautiful game', much of his upbringing is similar to mine, but it is his grappling with the interrelatedness of football, family and faith that really resonates with me. My hope is that as you read on, you too will gain insight and discover new depths of relationship way beyond football itself.

David Oakley, CEO and British Director, Ambassadors Football

Introduction

What a great day for football.
All we need is some green grass and a ball.

BILL SHANKLY, MANAGER OF LIVERPOOL FOOTBALL CLUB (1959–74)

The magic of football

My favourite radio programme is Radio 4's *Desert Island Discs*. In it, the interviewee chooses which songs, book and luxury item he or she would take to a desert island. To be invited on to the show is surely the loftiest ambition anyone could ever achieve. I'll probably never even get close, but it doesn't stop me planning my appearance—making mental lists of the discs I would select to take with me and thinking about what my luxury item would be. I often change my mind about my chosen discs and book; I never do about my luxury item. It is a ball.

I am fairly certain that soon after I entered this world I was given a ball—if not straight away, then without doubt within my first few years. I have owned hundreds of them since, and all have brought me immeasurable amounts of pleasure. I am no expert on the relative historical significance of items that have impacted the world, but I think the humble ball must be a contender for the best invention in the history of our planet. Neither do I know the origins of the ball in human history, but I reckon it is safe to attribute the original design to the architect of the universe: God himself. When he designed the planets he made them round. He understood the beauty and functionality of a ball, and now here we live with a ball always beneath our feet. Is it any wonder the sport of football has such a compelling and enthralling power over the human race?

A ball is a beautiful object. Perhaps its beauty comes from its simplicity. It is, after all, only air encased in a man-made skin, but then if you think about an opal or a ruby or a garnet it is, at its most basic, essentially just a lump of rock. We still look at such jewels with awe and admiration. We appreciate them because they are straightforward, easy to understand, easy to appreciate. A ball is the same; it is a jewel of a different sort.

A ball moves beautifully, like a graceful skater or a bird in flight, and it not only looks beautiful, it feels beautiful too. On the day I began to write this introduction I was in a park with my children. We had a ball and were kicking it around, watched keenly by a small boy barely a year old. It wasn't long before he toddled towards us with his eyes fixed on our ball. He pointed and said the word 'ball' as best he could. I got the impression it was one of only a few words he could say. I thought he might kick the ball, but he didn't. He bent down slowly, picked it up and simply held it reverentially, like a mother cradling a newborn baby. I could tell it felt good to him. He smiled.

A ball stimulates the senses from an early age and is accessible to all, regardless of age, race or affluence. There is a passage in the autobiography of the great footballer Pelé in which he describes some of the first footballs he played with:

We had to make do with stuffing paper or rags into a sock or stocking, shaping it as best we could into a sphere and then tying it with string. Every now and then we would come across a new sock or bit of clothing—sometimes, it must be said, from an unattended clothes line—and the ball would get a little bit bigger, and we'd tie it again. Eventually it came to resemble something close to a proper football.

Perhaps Pelé's testimony supports my theory that the human blueprint includes an instinct for a ball.

But it is not just the look or the feel or the movement of a ball that makes it such a profound item. It is what a ball can be used for, what it can achieve, that makes it such an outstanding example of ingenuity. In leading coaching sessions I often say to children, 'Put your foot on the ball,' or 'Hold the ball still,' but I am missing the point, which is that a ball is not meant to be kept still. A ball should be in motion and we are meant to move with it. A ball compels us to move; it heals us of our stagnation, and it rouses and warms our muscles. A ball causes us to smile and laugh and scream and giggle, and it leads us to communicate in a much deeper way than we do with mere words.

In the final scene of the film *Field of Dreams* (1989), the main character, Ray Kinsella, played by Kevin Costner, meets up with the ghost of his estranged father. Ray's wife says that she will leave them to talk and retreats to the house. Ray and his father exchange a few words before, struggling to control his emotion, Ray says to his father, 'Dad, you wanna have a catch?'

'I'd like that,' says Ray's father, and they pick up a baseball and simply throw it to one another. It is a poignant moment, a moving piece of film that shows us the power of a ball, as the childlike act of throwing it to one another begins to restore a relationship.

So there it is: my eulogy to the ball. The ball is an object that is accessible, functional and versatile. Frankly, it is a work of genius, and I have decided that I shan't be without one for as long as I live.

✤

PART 1

The soul of football

Walk on through the wind
Walk on through the rain
Tho' your dreams be tossed and blown.

FROM 'YOU'LL NEVER WALK ALONE',
FROM THE MUSICAL *CAROUSEL*

❖

CHAPTER 1

It all began in '65

Just after five o'clock on a Saturday afternoon in May 1965 the roofs were raised in roughly half the homes in Liverpool—the red half. They were mainly terraces and semis, but perhaps the odd detached house too. It was the moment that Liverpool's capture of the FA Cup, for the first time in their history, was sealed.

At full time the scores in the Wembley final were level: Liverpool 0, Leeds 0. Roger Hunt scored first in extra time to put Liverpool ahead. Billy Bremner levelled things just before the break and then, with only nine minutes of extra time remaining, Ian St John leapt up and headed the winning goal. As he jumped he seemed to contort his body in an unnatural way to get his head behind the ball, so that his feet and lower body remained in roughly the position he had launched from and his upper body and head twisted backward to reach the ball. It looked like a difficult posture to get into quickly and certainly an impossible position from which to power a ball from his forehead into the back of the Leeds net. But 'The Saint', as he was affectionately known, did it, and in the space of seconds became a Merseyside legend. As his reputation was established, my father and grandfather looked on in the Wembley stands—probably cheering and punching the air, and maybe even hugging each other.

But there were still nine minutes to go, and it was at this point, so The Saint says in his autobiography, that he suffered an attack of instant religion. 'Please, God, give me this,' he prayed, desperately wanting Liverpool to hang on until the full-time whistle. I doubt God would have taken much notice. I expect he may even have chuckled as he filed The Saint's appeal away under 'Inappropriate Prayers', along with all the other prayers said by footballers who had suddenly decided to open up a line of communication with him in similar situations. I guess there was probably a surge in messages to God from a certain stadium in London and a city in the north-west of England at the same time, all of which were filed alongside The Saint's plea. But I know there was at least one person at Wembley that afternoon who did not appeal to God. It was my father, and the reason for his silence was not that he didn't believe in God. In fact, it was the exact opposite. He knew God intimately, and his faith would not have been something he would ever have tried to use to further the fortunes of his beloved team. He knew such a prayer would have been futile anyway.

The FA Cup Final was not a game that could ever have been missed, but I missed it. I feel I had a good excuse, though: it was five years before I was born. Strangely, I still feel a little guilty. I dream of standing before Liverpool's saviour, Mr Bill Shankly, saying, 'I'm sorry for not being there, Sir. The only excuse I have is that I wasn't born,' and Shanks—the Scots authoritarian, master of the short, memorable response—saying, 'You should have been there anyway, son. You don't know what you missed.' He would have been right: I don't know what I missed. I can only imagine.

After the Liverpool players had taken the FA Cup on the traditional lap of honour and soaked up the crowd's adulation, after they had drunk champagne in the dressing room to toast their own success and posed for the press photographs, they passed a football around on which each player signed his name. I don't know when they actually did this, but I like to think that it was in the midst of the dressing-room celebrations when their hands were still muddy, their hearts were still pumping and the sweet taste of victory was still on their lips. It was more likely, though, to have been the following day on the return journey to Liverpool when the inevitable sense of anticlimax must have begun to kick in, when the flavour of winning had begun to taste bland, when plans had begun to germinate for the next conquest. Nevertheless, at some point the football was signed by the likes of Ron Yeats, Roger Hunt, Ian Callaghan and the hero himself, Ian St John.

Eventually the ball was raffled to raise money for charity and was won by a friend of my grandfather—a friend who felt he had a debt of gratitude to repay. He cancelled that debt by giving the football to my grandfather. And the gesture for which he felt he needed to say thank you? My grandfather, the chief steward at Anfield, had given him a job as a match-day steward—an undervalued, underpaid job, but nevertheless one that for thousands of people was only a dream. To be employed by Liverpool FC, no matter for what menial task, was a position to die for. This man's dream had come true thanks to my grandfather's typical generosity. My grandfather died when I was 13 years old, so I don't remember a lot about him, but I do know he was a kind man and he would not have expected to be thanked with a gift. But I'm glad he was.

My grandfather gave the football to my father, who gave it to me. I am looking at it now. The leather is brown and thick, the ball heavy. It feels real, natural and earthy. There is nothing synthetic about it. It does not stick to the palm of your hand like a modern ball, and there is little chance of anyone ever swerving it in the air in Beckham-esque fashion or daintily flicking it here and there like Cristiano Ronaldo. It is undoubtedly made for a straight, direct game—a game characterised by power, determination, dogged persistence and sheer willpower. This kind of football is still played every Saturday afternoon on muddy pitches up and down the country and in Sunday-afternoon-in-the-park kickabouts between dads and their lads. It is the type of football I grew up with.

To me, the signed Liverpool football isn't simply leather, stitching and the signatures of a whole team of legends. Its meaning is much more symbolic, because it represents a legacy passed down the generations of men in my family. This legacy is a love of football, and of Liverpool FC itself.

Nobody is in any doubt as to how important football was to Liverpool's charismatic manager Bill Shankly. Scan through the many books or websites devoted to what the man said, and you will quickly realise that football was, if not his top priority, very close to it. Football was his passion—pure and unbridled.

The day after the Cup Final the team were welcomed back to Liverpool by half a million people, and Shankly, never one for understatement, described it as 'the happiest day of my life'. Many of those fans would have felt the same. The long-awaited capture of a trophy that had eluded Liverpool for so long would have lifted the spirits of many people who, in their own humdrum lives, had very little to rejoice in.

Liverpool's achievement had united my grandfather and father in celebration, but I doubt they would have been quite as ebullient as Shanks in describing how it had impacted on their lives. Make no mistake—they were loyal and committed Liverpool supporters. My father, as well as my grandfather, stewarded at Anfield, and they would both have done so even if they had been required to pay for the privilege. The victory would have made them happy, but there were things in their lives more important to them than football. This point is illustrated by the fact that on the day after the Cup Final my father decided not to go to see Liverpool bring home the trophy and parade it around the city. He was to be married in a month to a woman who had no interest in football whatsoever—my mother—and after the previous day's trip to Wembley my father wisely chose to spend Sunday with her. But that makes it sound as though he decided not to go to witness the team's homecoming simply out of loyalty to my mother. I don't believe that was the case. It may have been difficult for fans with the same attitude as Bill Shankly to understand, but I think my father wanted to be with my mother on that day more than he wanted to join the vast throng of people helping Shanks celebrate the happiest day of his life.

In the competitive league of family, faith and football, football—though vitally important—would always come last, even if the great man Mr Shankly said it should be otherwise. My father's commitment to his faith and family exceeded all others. It was a principle that would find its way into my own life too.

✦

CHAPTER 2

Living with fairies in Kensington Gardens

I grew up quickly for a boy of my era. The milestones that typically mark the transition from being a boy to being a man came early for me: I left home when I was 19 years old; I was engaged and married when I was only 21; and my first child came along when I reached 26. Not that any of these events guarantees maturity, but in my case it was probably maturity that prompted these landmarks to occur earlier than they did for most of my peers. You see, 'mature' was a label I grew up with, and it was a mixed blessing. It helped me to attract much praise from adults. 'He's very sensible for his age,' they said. It was intended as a compliment, but I rarely took it as such. From the perspective of my friends, other than in unusual moments of seriousness, there was nothing admirable about being sensible. 'A nice, sensible lad' reputation was not a badge of honour a teenage boy would pin to his lapel and wear with pride. And so it was a difficult quality to bear, but I had no choice; it was, after all, my nature.

However, in one way I suffered from a Peter Pan complex, a monumental immaturity. In the story of Peter Pan, Peter explains to Wendy that he once overheard his mother and father talking about what he would be when he became a man. He didn't want to grow up; he wanted to be a child forever, so to avoid the fate his parents had in mind for him he ran away to live with fairies in Kensington Gardens. For many years I too lived with the fairies in Kensington Gardens because I held on to a childhood dream long after it was possible that it could ever become reality.

It was a dream I shared with the vast majority of other boys and men. The dream was fuelled by Subbuteo and *Match of the Day*, by Panini stickers and *Football Focus*, by *Match* magazine and football cards with flat, rigid pieces of bubble gum so sharp you could cut yourself if you put them into your mouth at the wrong angle. But most of all it was a dream fuelled by a man called Roy Race of Melchester Rovers, probably the greatest footballer never to have lived.

The highlight of my week was when my father returned from his trip to the newsagent's shop to pay for the papers on a Saturday morning with a copy of *Roy of the Rovers* tucked under his arm. It was a comic—but so much more than a mere comic too. It was a piece of inspirational literature, filling my head with ideas and hopes and dreams. I remember reading a story in which Roy Race honed his almost perfect dribbling ability by taking a football into a forest and weaving in and out of the mighty oaks with the ball glued to his feet. I could not wait to get into the woods behind our house to emulate my hero. It must have seemed very odd to the dog walkers and strolling couples to see a young lad trying to keep up with his football, diving into holly bushes to retrieve it and slipping and sliding in the mud. Roy Race made it look so simple.

For me, the most memorable storyline was the one in which, due to a sudden outbreak of illness, Melchester Rovers had too few players at the ground and had to resort to picking a fan from the crowd to play for them. They still won the game and the fan played so well that he earned himself a professional contract. It may not have been exactly like that, but that is the beauty of a story: you can use your imagination to make it your own, and make it my own I did.

My dream was to play for Liverpool FC, and if the opportunity to do so did not come through the normal channels there was always the hope that one wonderful day I might be picked out of the vast Anfield crowd to pull on the red shirt and score the winning goal for the best team in the world on the most hallowed turf on the face of the earth. And to the football-dreaming child that I was, this seemed a realistic possibility. I would not have accepted that being pulled from the crowd at Anfield was never, ever going to happen; if there was even the slightest chance, 45,000 spectators would turn up to every match with a pair of football boots in hand. But in my mind I was sure that if it had happened to a Melchester Rovers fan, it could happen to a Liverpool fan. I now just needed to calculate the chances of it occurring, so I decided to consult the definitive authority: Roy Race.

Fortunately for me, Roy answered questions, and even more thrilling was the fact that he answered them in print in the pages of his comic. I took up a fountain pen. Despite the difficulties those instruments caused me in my youth—leakages in pockets, splurges on the page and semi-permanently stained fingertips, to name just a few—

only a fountain pen would do for such an important task; a mere biro would not be at all appropriate for a letter to Roy. I needed to maximise my chances of getting a reply, and I was certain that a fountain pen would do the trick. Using immense concentration, after several drafts I had written a letter that, although it would never be preserved as having made a momentous contribution to the history of correspondence, would hopefully elicit a response. It went something like this:

Dear Roy,
Please could you tell me, what was the lowest attendance there has ever been at a football match? Thanks.

Yours sincerely,
Mark Chester

I was proud of that letter. I posted it and waited. Every week, I snatched the comic from my father as he returned from the newsagent's and, skipping all the stories I had up to that point always devoured in order, turned immediately to the letters page. After a few weeks of disappointment my glory moment arrived: my letter had been printed, and there below it in beautiful black ink, in the pages of the greatest sports literature ever produced, was my name. My name! I couldn't believe it. It was the proudest moment of my life. Roy Race had read my letter and replied, and in so doing had shared our correspondence with countless thousands of football fans across many different countries. I was speechless, breathless and fulfilled.

Quickly my mind turned to what Roy's answer might be. What were my chances of being pulled from a crowd to make my debut appearance for Liverpool? It was better than I had thought. To this day I cannot remember any of the details of Roy's reply—other than the most important of all: the number. It was a number that filled me with hope: the number 13. Only 13! The lowest attendance at a professional football match was only 13. Now I just needed a few circumstances to collide. Liverpool needed to be playing at home; I needed to be there; only twelve others needed to turn up to watch—all of them fat, old or useless at football; and an illness needed to sweep through the club and bring down all but ten of the players at the last minute. Completely impossible, you might say. But there was no space for impossibilities in my young brain; it was full of dreams that seemed entirely realistic—probable even.

As I got older my 'being pulled from the crowd' dream faded. I began to realise how fantastical it was, but my more mature mind was still dreaming. In fact, after an evening writing some of this chapter I went to bed and dreamt that after a one-two with Steven Gerrard I coolly placed the ball firmly in the back of the Kop goal. It was a fantastic feeling, and even though waking up and realising it had all been a dream brought me quickly down to earth again, it could not eliminate all of the pleasure I felt. Throughout the following day I occasionally broke into a smile just at the thought of it. What must it be like for real? A player like Lionel Messi must live in a permanent state of satisfaction.

I'm at risk of sounding a little childish, but I take some encouragement from an interview with a middle-aged Liverpool fan in which he says he can make himself go to sleep at night thinking of the roar of the Kop and fancying himself thundering down the wing with his stomach hanging over his shorts and scoring a vital goal. So it isn't only me, you see.

I was still hoping, way into my 20s, that I would one day play for Liverpool. Perhaps I was a late starter. I would be spotted playing in non-league football in my mid-20s and experience a meteoric rise to the Liverpool first team. It had happened to others. Or, if that didn't happen, a chance encounter with a Liverpool scout might result in a trial at which I would perform so well that a contract and a regular place in the side would follow.

That's the beauty of dreams: anything is possible. They can evolve and twist and turn. But the forlorn truth is that with advancing years we dream less and the dreams we hold dear begin to fade. We can then be left with disappointment, even resentment—but sometimes the death of a dream can turn out to be a surprisingly positive experience; it can be accompanied by the realisation that we would never have found what we were searching for in the place we hoped it would be. Our dreams would, in reality, never have given us the fulfilment we imagined they would bring. And when we let go of our dreams, which inevitably we often must do, we are sometimes surprised to discover that our fulfilment lies in a place as far removed from our original dream as it is possible to be.

My football story began with a dream of playing for

Liverpool Football Club at Anfield and it ended in a vastly different place—a place in which I discovered the true soul of football.

✣

CHAPTER 3

God speaks to my mother

I don't know much about what my father did in his job as a match-day steward at Anfield. It seems to be a common symptom of a son's relationship with his father that we never really ask much about our fathers' lives and they never really tell us, and then when we realise we are interested— in fact, desperate to know—it is too late and our fathers are gone. I am not sure why this is. Perhaps we worry that our fathers will be embarrassed to be asked about themselves, or maybe we mistakenly think that a man always wants to focus on the future and not keep being dragged back to his past, however happy or fulfilled it may have been.

However, I do know this: one of my father's duties on a match day was to hold open a door as the players ran past and out on to the pitch. What a tremendous privilege that must have been; I imagine it to be one of the most desirable duties a match-day steward could have had. At Anfield, for the players to get from their changing rooms to the pitch they first have to traverse the players' tunnel, which involves walking down a flight of steps below the 'This Is Anfield' sign, which the home players touch reverentially on their way to the pitch. At the bottom of the steps the players go through a door before climbing another flight of steps and running out while the crowd is in the middle of

31

a full-throated rendition of the club's anthem 'You'll Never Walk Alone'. It was this door that my father would hold open while handing footballs to the players as they ran past.

Years later, I had the opportunity to walk through this part of the ground and, noticing that someone had installed a simple hook and eye to hold the door back, I wondered if this had been my father's undoing. For a fraction of the fee they paid him to steward for one match the club had discovered an equally effective way of ensuring the players' safe passage to the pitch. I can't help but feel that my father got to carry out the privileged duty longer than could reasonably have been expected; it took the club quite a while to realise the benefits of the old-fashioned sort of hardware!

I know, though, that it wasn't the hook and eye that made my father leave his post at Anfield; it was God. When I was four years old God spoke to my mother, and the course of our lives changed significantly. I am aware that making such a statement will, in the minds of some, mark me out as a religious zealot, out of touch with reality. But I have to assure you that I do not speak about the divine voice as lightly as others might. Sometimes it seems, from the way people speak, as though they have a daily dialogue with the Almighty. My conversational relationship with God is less clear. Hearing from God is shrouded with doubt and uncertainty, and my faith life is a constant quest to hear and understand what he might be saying. I ask him to speak, but I don't often hear, and I wonder whether he is a mute God or I am a deaf child. But when God does speak I know it is important; the words of a silent one are all the more precious for the wait. I believe my mother and father have had similar struggles in trying to hear God, but there was no doubt in their minds—and I am certain too, having heard the story—that on this occasion God spoke very clearly to my mother.

It does not surprise me that it was my mother to whom God chose to convey his message. When God speaks and wants to be heard, it is only natural for him to choose a good listener to communicate with, and my mother has always been a good, conscientious listener. Her listening at times is intense; she does not just want to hear, she wants to understand, and not just what a person is saying but why they are saying it. Hearing the words is window shopping. My mother wants to be inside the shop searching through the clothes rails in the furthest, most obscure nooks and crannies of the store.

As far as I am aware, my mother has never had any formal training to be an 'active listener' or 'counsellor', and yet she is the most natural counsellor I have ever met. Training would have spoilt her. Training helps to activate a dormant skill or develop it to the maximum of its potential, but in doing so it can constrain a person; it can dull creativity and shackle initiative. Football is a great example. Coaching can bring the best out of a player who has limited ability, but take a young player who is naturally gifted and train him using the latest theory, give him a position and tell him to stick to it, give him the ball and tell him never to risk losing it, and you might end up with a player who is a fantastic technician but has lost his creative flair. It would be like training van Gogh to be a painter and decorator. Why teach someone how to decorate perfectly, when, left alone, they could paint portraits and landscapes so stunning they would take a person's breath away? Van Gogh's art was painting pictures; Kenny Dalglish's art was playing football; my mother's art is listening. And so it was that the only time in my family's history that I can say with certainty that God spoke to us, he chose my mother to receive his message.

It was late 1974 and my father had escaped the confines of a shipping company office to retrain as a probation officer. It was a career move prompted by an old football teammate of my father—a man called Dave Weedall. He had simply cut out a newspaper advertisement for jobs in the probation service and sent it to my father. Maybe it was God leading him to do so, because certainly Dave was a man of faith. My father tells a story about an incident on the football field when they played together for St Leonard's, Bootle in the local league. One of the opposition had been seriously injured in a tackle. As everyone crowded around the unfortunate victim, Dave had wandered over and loudly suggested—in all seriousness—that the St Leonard's team should lay hands on the poor lad and pray for healing. Wisely, he was dissuaded, and they waited for God's healing touch to arrive in the more worldly form of an ambulance. This tale makes my father chuckle every time he retells it. It was a coincidence—one that demonstrated the often apparent circularity of life—that, when I reached 19, and the world of work, the first office I worked in contained none other than Dave Weedall. He was to his credit still a man who brought his faith to bear in everyday situations without an ounce of hesitation or embarrassment.

After a year's training—including three months of travelling between Liverpool and London, where he carried out some of his studies—my father qualified as a probation officer and was appointed to the North Wales Service. My mother and father looked at a house in North Wales, in a village just outside a town called Holywell, and my father was certain that it was the place for his young family to set up their new home. My mother was more cautious and wanted confirmation that this was going to be the right place to live, so she asked the person she was sure would know what would be best.

My mother faithfully observed a regular time of quiet prayer and reflection. She used a small black book called *Daily Light* to guide her to some chosen words from the Bible and to amplify the message they contained. I cannot recall ever seeing her during her quiet times; they would have been intensely private moments. But her Bible and the *Daily Light* book were always beside her bed, so I know they were, and still are, dear to her. I can imagine her now in one of those quiet times, asking God for some guidance. Perhaps it was a simple prayer, something like 'Father God, please show me if this is the right place for my family'. Whatever words she used, God heard them, and not long afterwards he answered her prayer.

Every week my mother would meet up with a small group of other young mums from the Liverpool neighbourhood in which we used to live. They would meet at the home of one of the women, and the children would play while the adults' conversations centred on sleep patterns, speech development, eating habits and behavioural traits. These young mums also had something else in common; they all believed in God. So at some point during their get-together the conversations would stop and they would have an epilogue. One or two would read from the Bible and share their thoughts, while others would recount experiences in which they felt God had helped or encouraged them. Then several of the women would pray. At one of the meetings, soon after my mother had appealed to God for guidance, one of the young mums said she felt compelled to read out a passage from the book of Isaiah, chapter 35. The reading began:

The desert and the parched land will be glad;
   the wilderness will rejoice and blossom.
Like the crocus, it will burst into bloom;
   it will rejoice greatly and shout for joy.
The glory of Lebanon will be given to it,
   the splendour of Carmel and Sharon;
they will see the glory of the Lord,
   the splendour of our God.

ISAIAH 35:1–2

It might seem to you that the words are fairly innocuous—typical biblical language and little in the way of guidance about moving to a house in North Wales—but this passage contained a message: a reply from God to my mother. You see, the house my parents had looked at and were agonising over was in a village called Carmel, and the name of the house, displayed on a wooden name plate alongside the front door, was Sharon. My mother was certain God had spoken to her, because not a single one of the other people in the room that day had known that the village my parents had visited was called Carmel or that the house they had viewed was named Sharon—so that particular Bible passage being chosen and read out was either an incredible and unbelievable coincidence or it was inspired by God.

My mother was now convinced. We packed up and followed God's leading to Carmel and Sharon, the house that would become the Chester family home for the next three decades. At the time, and still to some extent today, North Wales was considered by most Liverpudlians to be an extraordinary distance away. For a start, it was 'over the water', meaning that it was on the wrong side of the River Mersey, and, secondly, it was a different country filled with 'woolly backs', a strange species of people who actually chose to live outside of a city. North Wales is now less than an hour's drive from Liverpool; maybe it was more in the early 1970s, but anyway a decision was made to move house. I don't think it is too strong to say that some members of the family regarded this as an act of desertion. But my mother had sought God's guidance, and he had answered her, so we had to act.

After travelling from North Wales to Liverpool to steward at Anfield on match days for a few years, my father felt that it was becoming too much. His family was getting older and something had to give. Of course, his family came first and so he resigned his stewarding position. It was not too long, though, before he would take up a different footballing pursuit to fill his vacant Saturdays—one that he would enjoy with his sons.

✣

— CHAPTER 4 —

Joey speaks to my father

In the 1970s and 80s, fêtes were an important part of life in the North Wales countryside. They were significant social occasions, and, given the not unreasonable distance to the surrounding villages, it was possible to visit one practically every weekend of the summer months. A fête created an enormous amount of excitement in my young heart, not least because it contained the altogether thrilling prospect of winning a goldfish—if I could only achieve the apparently almost impossible task of throwing a ping-pong ball into a jam jar. In fact, it was the anticipation of success that made fêtes so enticing. There were so many chances to win something. It might be a few extra pennies on the 'roll the penny' stall, a bottle of something illicit on the tombola, a whistle in the lucky dip or someone's unwanted Christmas chocolates in the raffle. But none was as good as the elusive jackpot that was the goldfish. I desperately wanted to win a goldfish. I imagined myself proudly carrying away a plastic bag containing my new orange friend swimming happily in a thimbleful of water. Alas, it was never to be. My hand–eye coordination was simply not up to scratch.

My first experience of a fête came early on in our new life in Carmel. It took place in a nearby village called Pantasaph, which was dominated by and renowned locally for its friary.

This friary was home to none other than Father Francis, the internationally acclaimed singing friar and local hero, who, despite selling records around the world, still had the humility to play his guitar and sing for people's pleasure on the streets of Holywell, the town around which our villages were clustered.

The friary fascinated me and my friends. It looked and felt and was so different from what we understood from our experience of life. It held promises of something that was outside the world we knew. For a start, the people who inhabited it dressed oddly. Their dull brown smocks and open-toed sandals set them apart from your average inhabitant of our area. North Wales, in the 1970s and 1980s, could not be said to be the fashion capital of the world—for example, our choice of sporting footwear was limited to plain black plimsolls or the slightly more sophisticated Adidas Kick trainers—but the friars were still way behind the rest of us. Secondly, the friars lived in a most enormous building on the side of a hill, surrounded by what seemed then to be a huge forest, which they owned. Coachloads of pilgrims came to visit the friary. They would make their slow and steady way into the forest to meander reverentially through the trees, pausing at the twelve stations of the cross before reaching the summit of the hill and the statue of Christ hanging on the cross. Then they would bow their heads in the small chapel at the foot of the cross, light their candles and make their way quietly down the hill and back to their coaches.

The grounds of the friary were skirted by a six-foot wall, but from the fields in which we played we could see the back of the cross on which Christ was hanging. Naturally, from time to time, our curiosity would get the better of us and we would decide to take a closer look. One of us would be hoisted to the top of the wall by the rest to make sure that the coast was clear, and, having been given the signal, we would all clamber over the wall to gaze at Christ in his glorious moment. We were fascinated and horrified. This was not like the crucifixes worn by people around their necks—tiny and toy-like. This was life-size and looked so real. Next, one person would stand as lookout while the rest of us entered the chapel. We would snoop around before sitting for a while in silence. The lookout would then be relieved, to give him a chance to snoop around with us. Once everyone had had their fill of religious trespassing, we would climb back over the wall, resolving to bring matches next time so that we could light candles too.

The whole experience felt illicit. We felt we were doing something wrong. We felt we were where we should not have been and yet—unlike other illicit pursuits—there was something strangely fulfilling about our excursions to the foot of the cross. We went with respect and curiosity; there was never any intention to do damage, and the feel of the place dulled our natural rowdiness. Faced with people whose lives we did not understand, we could respond in one of two ways: with fear or with curiosity. Had we reacted with fear, we might have avoided the friars and their home, or we might have attacked them and their way of life by vandalising what we saw. But we didn't; we just wanted to know more about them. Anyway, once a year they provided us with a chance to win a goldfish, so we owed them. You see, it was the friars who arranged and hosted the Pantasaph fête.

So, early on in our new life as a family in North Wales, we took advantage of the friars' hospitality and visited their fête—my mother, father, older brother Stephen and me. I was six years old and feeling a little nervous at the number of people filtering into the fields on which the fête was taking place. We wandered about from stall to stall, and as our parents chatted to people they met, Stephen and I took the opportunity to calculate to which stalls we would return to spend our pennies. As the afternoon progressed, every now and then I spotted a child holding a bag containing the most beautiful and fascinating treasure: a live goldfish. I decided that this would be my afternoon's objective. If nothing else, I had to win a goldfish. But first there was an attraction even more enthralling to visit—one at which some profound words were spoken that would leave an impression on me for the rest of my life.

In a corner of the field stood a man with whom you could pose for a photograph. This was no ordinary man, however. He was a Liverpool player—a resolute left back and an endearing character by the name of Joey Jones. He was a son of the parish of North Wales and was attending the fête to meet up with his compatriots, chat, sign autographs and smile for picture after picture after picture. As a family, we decided that meeting Jones was a priority, so this would be our first stop. We made our way over to join the queue, but as we approached the great man something startling happened. It caused me to stop and stare with my jaw slightly dropped, and years later I can still recall the incident with great clarity. Jones looked up from scrawling his name in a child's autograph book, saw my father and said, 'Hello, John!' Only two small words but, for me, they contained extraordinary significance.

Firstly, Jones had felt that my father was of sufficient importance to pick him out of a crowd and say 'Hello' directly to him. That alone would have considerably swelled my admiration for my father. But Jones did not just say 'Hello'; he said, 'Hello, John!' Joey Jones knew my father's name! I was astounded and thrilled. I had thought my family was an ordinary one, living in an ordinary house in an ordinary village, with the children of the family attending an ordinary school and the father in an ordinary job. How wrong I had been! All of a sudden I realised that we were not ordinary after all. Ordinary families were not recognised in the midst of a crowd by famous footballers. Ordinary families did not cause proceedings at the local fête's 'Photo with Famous Footballer' stand to come to a halt while the famous footballer in question chatted away with the head of the family (as my father had now, in my eyes, clearly become). We were a special family, one associated with greatness, and I was proud. Clearly, my father had the perfect pedigree for what he was about to become. He had time (now his Saturdays were free), he had experience at a First Division football club (albeit as a steward), and he knew professional players.

My brother Stephen and I rather nervously took up our positions on either side of Jones and tried to smile without revealing our anxiety. The photograph was taken. With a shake of his hand, Joey Jones said goodbye to my father and that he would see him again soon, and we wandered off to the other activities. I don't remember much about the fête after that. However, apart from the words spoken between my father and Jones, two things about that day have stayed in my memory.

One, my mother had no idea who Joey Jones was.

Two, I did not win a goldfish that day, but my brother won two.

Life is often mystifying and very unfair.

— CHAPTER 5 —

My brother speaks to the nation

When I was eight my playing career began in humble surroundings with the 1st Carmel Cub Scout Group football team. We changed in the village hall and trekked across the road to the school football pitch, which sloped considerably from wing to wing. The manager of the team was a man whose commitment and dedication to us young lads I took for granted for many years, but for whom my admiration and respect would grow as I matured. The manager was my father. After leaving Liverpool Football Club he enthusiastically seized the opportunity to move into the precarious world of football management. It could be said that with the 1st Carmel Cub Scouts he started at the bottom, but an accusation that could never be levelled at him was that he failed to take his responsibility as a football manager seriously. I cannot remember him giving anything less than 100 per cent to his young protégés. It could be argued, however, that at times his dedication went a little too far.

The 1st Carmel Cub Scout Group football team played its matches on Saturday mornings. One January Friday we had fairly heavy snowfall—perhaps a couple of inches—so the prospects of a match on the Saturday were not looking good. We lads looked forward to Saturday all through the week. Analysis of the last game and anticipation of the next gave us a topic of conversation to brighten those long days in the classroom at Carmel County Primary School. We were always disappointed if a match ever got postponed— but not as disappointed as my father. Most managers of junior football teams would relish the odd occasion a match was postponed. They would enjoy the chance to have an unscheduled lie-in or catch up on those long-standing DIY jobs. Not my father. He loathed anything that prevented football being played, so on this particular Friday he decided that he would not be beaten by a couple of inches of snow; come what may, the game would go ahead. He phoned around the lads and asked them and their parents to arrive a couple of hours early on Saturday morning, with spades and shovels. We were going to clear the snow off the pitch in time for kick-off.

I can imagine the phone call on the Friday night from the manager of the opposing team.

'Hello, John. It's Mike here from 6th Rhyl. I've not heard from you, but I assume the game's off in the morning.'

'No, the match is still on, Mike.'

'But, John, there are a couple of inches of snow on the ground.'

'Not on our pitch there isn't, Mike, or should I say there won't be by kick-off. It's all sorted. The game's on.'

I am glad the slope on our pitch meant it drained well, otherwise he would have had us out after heavy rainfall with extension leads and hairdryers!

After four years of playing for the Cubs I reached the age to move on. Coincidentally—or so I thought at the time—

my father began a new football team: Carmel Juniors Under-12s. It was around this time that a new player of exceptional quality joined our ranks. His name was Andrew Emslie. He quickly became known as Ems, because no one in a football team is ever called by their proper name. Everyone must have a nickname. Unfortunately, we footballers are not the most imaginative when it comes to wordplay, so the general rule for devising football nicknames is, if possible, to add a 'y' to the surname, so Jones becomes Jonesy and Smith becomes Smithy. If a 'y' doesn't fit, try another letter. For example, someone with the surname Finn becomes Finno. It might be necessary to knock off a few letters before the new extension is applied, such as when Thomas becomes Tommo or, in my case, Chester becomes Chezzie. The next option is to shorten the surname, hence Emslie becoming Ems. It is only the truly privileged who get nicknames that are not variations of their surname, and usually it is because they look like someone else—generally someone famous and ugly. No one in a football team would ever get called Clooney, but they might get called Shrek!

Ems was widely regarded as the best footballer our part of North Wales had ever produced. He was a prolific goalscorer, and his was the name on the lips of all the First Division teams' scouts. He was destined for professionalism, and somehow my father managed to convince him to join Carmel Juniors. I can vividly remember Ems's first training session. It was the end of the summer and he had just returned from a holiday abroad. His skin was the colour of conkers, or so it seemed, because he wore a brilliant-white kit: pure white shirt, impeccable white shorts and spotless white socks. There was something celestial about the way he looked, and to this day I credit Ems's appearance at that first training session with my lifelong admiration for Real Madrid in their sublime all-white strip.

Ems looked awesome, and we were all intimidated by his presence. It quickly became evident that he was not only streets ahead of the rest of us in his fashion sense, but he was also on a different planet in terms of his football ability. He was quick, he was composed, the ball stuck to his feet like a barnacle and he was lethal in front of the goal. We were glad he was in our team.

Ems became a good friend of mine, and he and his beautiful wife, Nancy, remain treasured friends to this day. Many of my early football experiences were shared with Ems, but his trajectory—defined by his vastly superior talent—was very different from mine, and it is a regret that I have not played football with him since we were both 18. He no longer plays competitive football, but he has not abandoned his sartorial elegance and is still always the best-dressed man in any room. Very appropriately, when I married Su, Ems turned up to the wedding in a stunning, very expensive suit in a colour that perfectly complemented his tan. Yes, it was all white!

When I turned 13 my father launched a new branch of the Carmel Juniors Football Club—the Under-14s. Our Saturday football matches started to become a wider family affair for us because my brother Stephen began to referee. Stephen had neither the balance nor the coordination to make a great footballer, but he had perfect attributes for refereeing. He was decisive and single-minded and he couldn't have cared less what people thought about him. In describing him as such, I know I risk making him sound arrogant, but nothing could have been further from the truth. Attitudes towards him were overwhelmingly respectful. Even when he was a young lad, people—both peers and adults— thought highly of him. I can recall only one instance when somebody sought to bad-mouth my brother, and even that was half-hearted.

One night after school I had finished my tea and arrived at the school football pitch for a kickabout with my mates. A small crowd had gathered at one of the goalposts, and I was called over to witness the spectacle. The atmosphere was subdued, and the lads looked embarrassed and a little nonplussed. I quickly saw why that was: somebody had written graffiti on the goalpost and it was directed at my brother. Vandalism of this sort was not a particularly unusual sight in our area, but it was the nature of it that was surprising. In the normal course of events, somebody would take revenge for being wronged by scrawling something like 'Terry Williams is a ******!' on as public a surface as they could find. On this occasion, however, the insult was written in small and very neatly formed letters. It said, 'Stephen Chester still reads Enid Blyton's *Famous Five*!' Nobody could quite work out whether it was an attempt at abuse or a statement of admiration. We wandered away from the goalpost in silence and got on with our game of football. A few days later the posts were repainted by Clwyd County Council workmen and nothing more was ever said about the matter. Stephen's reputation remained unsullied and, after such a monumental misjudgement, the person responsible for the graffiti must have given up his deviant behaviour, because no such disparaging defacements—neat, polite and perfectly punctuated—appeared in our village again.

As a young referee, Stephen's main challenge was not dealing with dangerous tackling or player dissent. It was coping with the attitudes of the watching parents, as he once explained to the nation on primetime television. Among Stephen's many achievements is a feat which, at the time, made the whole family very proud. It was an accomplishment many families aspired to for their teenage children. But in our family it actually happened and Stephen did it. He appeared on the 1980s children's TV game show *Blockbusters*—a quiz in which a single player competed against a team of two by answering questions to win control of lettered hexagons and create a path of connecting hexagons across a game board. The programme was presented by the legendary Bob Holness. The show's most memorable line was uttered when a contestant chose the next lettered hexagon to go for by asking, 'Can I have a "P" please, Bob?' This of course amused children up and down the land every time it was said. Stephen didn't get a chance to ask for a 'P' because he was knocked out in his first game. We rallied as a family and stuck to the line that he had known all the answers, but just could not buzz fast enough. Admitting failure in speed of response was preferable to conceding any lack of knowledge. Even though he didn't last long, he did have time to explain to Bob that one of his pastimes—refereeing—was marred by the misbehaviour of parents on the touchline. He did not go as far as naming the culprits, but I think things eased up for him a little after he had expressed his plight to the whole country. His tormentors were temporarily shamed into silence.

As we got older, my father led his beloved team into the Under-16s league and our most successful season, the culmination of which was a narrow cup-final win over Oakenholt Gunners, our arch rivals. I cannot recall anything about the game—the score, the goalscorers or how I played—but I do remember that my father jubilantly bear-hugged every member of the team after the final whistle. It is funny how the seemingly important aspects of an event fade quickly from the memory, while the apparently inconsequential details turn out to have more enduring significance and are recalled more clearly as time passes.

My father's moment had come to hang up his manager's sheepskin jacket and return to shopping with my mother on Saturday afternoons. He had looked after the team for eight years and could now retire, basking in the glory of winning the trophy that took pride of place on top of our television. I imagine my mother was pleased that the dominance of Saturday football had come to an end, and work on the eight-year-old list of DIY tasks in the house could now be resumed. However, she did not count on what would happen next.

One day the phone rang, and it was the chairman of Rhyl Football Club for my father. He had heard of the reputation of the Carmel Juniors Under-16s team, and he wondered if my father would consider taking his players to the coast, where they would represent Rhyl FC as their youth team with my father as manager. My father was mentally brushing the dust off his sheepskin jacket before he had even put the phone back in its cradle.

Excitement rippled through our village and the lads were thrilled and apprehensive in equal measure. Rhyl Football Club was a proper football club with its own pitch, stands, floodlights and bar. The first team was in the Northern Premier League and people paid to watch them. They even had semi-professional players!

We practised together with the reserves and first team twice a week. Pre-season training was the toughest we had ever experienced, but we were filled with hope, excitement and expectation—and we were not disappointed. We started well in the league and progressed through the first round of the FA Youth Cup by beating Atherton Town in a replay at Rhyl's ground, Belle Vue. We faced Burton Albion away in the next round and were narrowly beaten, watched by the biggest crowd we had ever played in front of; there must have been over 100 paying spectators! I played for the reserve team a few times and was delighted to receive money for the expenses I incurred, which amounted to the grand total of zero, unless you included the Mars bar for the journey home!

It started to feel as if I was moving in the right direction and that a footballing career would not be impossible. Unfortunately, as the season progressed, things began to deteriorate for the Rhyl youth team. Alcohol and girls became bigger priorities for some of our players, and my father became increasingly disillusioned with having to phone round and rally half-committed players on Friday nights, and then drive to their homes on Saturday lunchtimes to rouse them from their hangovers. At the end of the season, my father again decided to end his managerial career, and this time it was for good.

During the summer, it would be fair to say that the phone was not hot with clubs asking me to play for them, so with no other option available to me—other than not playing—I took up a friend's invitation to join him at a team called Rhyl Victory Club. There were some decent footballers in the team, but I soon discovered that their love of kicking a ball around a football pitch was matched by their love of another Saturday-afternoon activity on a football field—fighting.

In the space of a few months my prospects of becoming a professional footballer had plummeted, and things would get even worse. It was during this season that something happened which caused me to lose my love of football completely.

— **CHAPTER 6** —

Losing my love of football

If I'm being honest, I cannot really remember much about John McBrien before the time we both entered the sixth form at Holywell High School, but we were to become good friends. Looking back now, I realise that in a couple of ways we were similar to each other, which was maybe what drew us together. We were both different from many of the lads around us and had interests that were not really deemed cool by our football-obsessed mates. I had a deeply held Christian faith and John—or Cotchy, as he was known (I have no idea why)—was a member of the local amateur dramatics society. Worshipping God and prancing about onstage in costumes were viewed with equal disdain. But while our chosen activities may have provoked a little mirth among our peers, I think the fact that we were both prepared to be slightly different caused others to respect us— even if, being typical teenage boys, they rarely expressed it. Certainly, Cotchy was esteemed; he was sociable and had many friends, and I admired his ability to remain true to himself and, at the same time, maintain his popularity. Inwardly, I agonised over my failure to be one of the crowd. I found the whole experience of being an unusual sort of teenage lad painful, but Cotchy never seemed to experience the same turmoil and consequent lack of self-confidence. He was his own person, comfortable in his own skin, and never felt the need to conform just to fit in, which was perhaps why he was so well liked. A good illustration of his single-mindedness was that at our weekly games of football he remained completely unmoved by his fellow players' fierce criticism and complaints when he would not pass the ball—which was 100 per cent of the time! With good nature he just ignored them or laughed off their outbursts of anger. The occasional goals he scored more than made up for the abuse he had to shrug off. I was more sensitive and eager to please.

The other similarity Cotchy and I had was that we both loved Liverpool FC, and although I do not think it was our passion for the club that made us friends, it certainly gave us something to talk about on our walks home from school. Cotchy had a great knowledge of football and an unshakable confidence in his opinions. This could have made him cocky, but nothing could be further from the truth. Cotchy simply possessed self-assurance beyond his years. It was perhaps his interest in politics that gave him his surety of opinion and ability to express it; but whatever the cause, he knew his own mind. I, on the other hand, was beset with doubts and found the arguments of others so persuasive that I became increasingly reluctant to express a view for fear of being exposed as an intellectual weakling. An indication of our character differences is that, all these years later, I can still remember which Reds player Cotchy argued was the greatest—Jan Molby—but I have not a clue which player I rated most highly at the time.

As our friendship grew, I discovered that Cotchy was a member of the Flintshire branch of the Liverpool

Supporters' Club, and I was delighted to hear that a coach of local Liverpool fans—Cotchy always in their midst—went to every match. I quickly joined and regularly began to make the journey over to Anfield to join the throng of supporters on the Kop, swaying and surging our way through matches. Like Cotchy, I loved watching Liverpool play but, unlike Cotchy's, mine was not a love that made me forsake all others, because my heart was first and foremost devoted to playing the game.

It was our contrasting priorities—Cotchy's to watch football, mine to play football—that took our paths in different directions on 15 April 1989. As usual, only a little earlier, Cotchy had said goodbye to his mother and father as he left his house that Saturday morning. He was on his way to join his mates on the Supporters' Club coach destined for Sheffield Wednesday's ground, Hillsborough, to watch Liverpool take on Nottingham Forest in the FA Cup semi-final. Some hours later, football boots in hand, I climbed into the car with my father. I was playing in a match that afternoon in Rhyl, and he was coming to watch. It was a typical Rhyl Victory Club match: banter in the dressing rooms, a few scuffles on the pitch, a couple of yellow cards and some goals in our favour. My father was on the line making his usual mental notes of what the team were doing wrong, ready to point them out to me at half-time, but he was distracted. He had a radio in his hand and was listening to the semi-final commentary through an earpiece. As I walked off the pitch for half-time, he looked worried. 'There's a problem at Hillsborough,' he said. 'It sounds like crowd trouble. People are getting crushed and the match has been stopped.'

In the 1980s, crowd trouble was not unusual in English stadiums. I had witnessed fighting between supporters myself, so at that stage I was not unduly troubled, and I returned to the pitch for the second half without a second thought. As the afternoon progressed, though, my anxiety grew. I could see my father becoming more agitated on the touchline, and I knew that what was happening in Sheffield was not just a few ripped-out seats and a half-hearted pitch invasion. It was something more serious.

By the time the referee blew the final whistle, I had long since lost interest in playing football. Despite being in the middle of a match, everyone involved somehow felt the same rising tension as the rest of the country. When something bad happens—something really bad—the usual atmosphere of everyday life is slowly but palpably smothered by an increasingly heavy blanket of apprehension and despair. At times, bad news seems to seep into the very bones of the nation. We just know something is wrong. On that football pitch in Rhyl we knew that something terrible was unfolding, and as we left the field our fears were confirmed: stories were emerging that lives had been lost in the crush at Hillsborough.

It is perhaps difficult to fully comprehend now, but even in those pre-internet times news travelled fast, and it was word of mouth that carried it rather than our current preference of text on screens. Eyewitness reports led to radio and television broadcasts, which led to conversations. We relied more on the people around us for our current affairs than on the army of journalists we now depend on. And the words coming from the people on the playing fields in Rhyl were horrifying.

I changed quickly, and my father and I headed for home in silence as we listened to the increasingly sombre radio broadcast. When we arrived home, we watched aghast the pictures and reports on television as the toll of confirmed deaths steadily rose. I am not sure when I started to become concerned about Cotchy. At first, my young mind probably just did not make the required connections to appreciate that he might have been caught up in the tragedy. Perhaps I had been blinded by the young person's belief in the invincibility of fellow young people. But at some point worry clasped me, and its grip got ever tighter as the evening progressed. By the time I picked up the telephone and dialled Cotchy's number I was seriously apprehensive, but also looking forward to hearing that he had arrived home and dispelling at least the very personal element of my anxiety about the day's events.

Cotchy's brother, Andrew, answered the telephone. It was a very brief call—one I guess he had repeated many times that evening, and that was mirrored in many other households. In a voice infused with desperation Andrew told me that no news had been received; they were still trying to make contact with Cotchy. This was before the era of mobile communications, so a lack of phone contact in the midst of the terrible confusion after an event of this magnitude— even five or six hours later—was not cause to give up hope. However, both Andrew and I knew, without saying so, that no news was increasingly likely to be bad news.

In the two decades that have passed since Hillsborough I have gone over these events time and time again, not trying to make sense of them—because there is no sense to be made—but just because I cannot get away from them. They are too horrific to think about and yet too horrific not to think about. However, until writing these words it had never dawned on me that when I telephoned Cotchy's house that evening, the shrill ringing would have given the whole family a brief moment of hope: could it be their beloved son and brother to say he was safe? I had never realised until now that, while my concern might have been appreciated, the sound of my voice would have increased their despair tenfold. Every call they received that was not from Cotchy would be like—and I hesitate to use this analogy because it is so appropriate—another nail in his coffin.

After a night of prayer and fitful sleep, I phoned back the following morning and spoke to Cotchy's brother again. His voice was a whisper. Cotchy would not be returning home; he was dead. His family was irreparably broken, and I had lost a special friend. I put down the receiver and cried.

— CHAPTER 7 —

The fall at Jericho

Just over a week later, with five of his other friends, I had the unhappy privilege of carrying Cotchy to his grave. A week after that, I did what I had always done on a Saturday: I played football. I was back playing for Rhyl Victory Club, and again my father came to watch. At the end of the match I changed quickly and walked back to the car with him. We both got in, and as soon as I had shut the door, I broke down in tears. Playing football that day had been an ordeal, and my relationship with the game was at an end. I had fallen out of love with it. It had taken my good and loyal friend, and I missed him.

When our love for something or somebody dies, there is a period in which we continue to act as though our feelings are unchanged. Unconsciously, perhaps, we pretend we still love that thing or person and continue to behave as we have always done. Maybe it is denial or simply habit that causes us to carry on saying the things we have always said and doing the things we have always done—or it could be hope that the feeling of love will return. It is not an entirely misplaced hope, because sometimes the feelings, prompted by the actions, do eventually return. I do not know why I carried on playing football after Cotchy died. I may have been in denial or I could have been hoping that my love for the game would return, but really I suspect it was just plain habit; I did not know how to spend Saturdays in any other way.

As for my faith in God, it was unaffected. On this occasion I did not question God or get angry with him or blame him. To me, what happened to Cotchy at Hillsborough did not seem to have anything to do with God. He did not cause this tragedy to happen; it was we humans. Blaming God would have been like blaming the inventor of the motor car for every fatal road traffic accident. So I prayed for Cotchy's family, for the families of all the other dead and injured, for the injured themselves and for myself. I needed God more than ever before.

I played out what little was left of the season with Rhyl Victory Club, and the following campaign I signed for a team called Halkyn to turn out for their reserves. Halfway through the season, in January, I moved to live in a bedsit in Liverpool to begin my career with HM Customs and Excise. I had been seduced by pictures of customs boats cutting through wild seas and thoughts of chasing drug smugglers in the glamorous style of my favourite television programme, *Miami Vice*. What I got was a desk job in the offices of the headquarters responsible for the administration of VAT.

Each weekend I would travel back from Liverpool to North Wales to stay with my mother and father, and on Saturday afternoons I continued to play for Halkyn until the season ended. By the time the new season kicked off, I had decided that I needed to stay in Liverpool at the weekends and continue my flagging and forlorn football career with a team near to my austere living accommodation—a team called St Mary's Old Boys. It was a decision prompted not least by the fact that I had found a new love in the bright lights of the big city.

At the warm and welcoming St Luke's Parish Church in Crosby, which I was now attending on Sundays, I had met a pretty, bubbly, ever-smiling redhead called Su Lucas, who shared my faith in God and, to a certain extent, my enjoyment of football. Her enthusiasm and positivity were infectious and absorbing—and she quickly became a rather welcome distraction from my sporting pastimes. She would watch me play football and then take me to her lively family home for tea, which was provided by her mother, Marg, in the form of roast dinners and the Liverpool speciality, scouse (a very thick stew with the delectable finishing touch of a pastry crust). Su's grandmother, Nell, began to wash my sports kit, using the most fragrant conditioner I have ever smelt, and Su's father, Tommy, lent me his car—even though, in his view, I supported the wrong football team (he has been visiting Goodison Park to watch Everton FC for over 50 years). Clearly, with this sort of attention, I decided early on that I would be marrying into the Lucas family and, fortunately, two years later Su agreed to have me. It was quite a surprise to find only a few months later that our decision to get married had catapulted us into the media spotlight and made us local celebrities. Su entered and won the *Crosby Herald* Bride of the Year competition, and I was consigned to the status of 'bridal accessory of the year', being required to spend a significant proportion of my spare time fulfilling my obligations to the competition's various sponsors by posing for photographs alongside my glamorous fiancée.

Although playing football was providing relief from the whirlwind of the Crosby celebrity circuit, I was beginning to realise that my footballing days were numbered. I no longer loved playing—I was doing it out of habit—and my performance on the pitch was not improving. On moving to Chester, our namesake city, after our marriage, I called a halt to kicking a ball about on a Saturday afternoon and replaced it with shopping, DIY and the privilege of spending time with the increasingly endearing *Crosby Herald* Bride of the Year.

It was a few years before my love of football would begin to spark into life again. Perhaps absence had made my heart grow fonder, but it was more likely that I had found a bunch of people I wanted to spend time with who happened to play football. After moving to Chester, Su and I tried several churches and eventually settled at Hoole Baptist Church. We rapidly fell in with a group of people of a similar age to us who were sincere in their faith in God. I eventually became aware that some of the younger men who were joining our church were connected with men from other Chester churches by their passion for football. They played each week and, led by Dave Evans, a humble but visionary man, had formed themselves—appropriately for a Christian team—into Crossway FC. The men of Chester—and a considerable number of the children and women too—have much to thank Dave for, because Crossway FC has given hundreds, if not thousands, of people the chance to indulge in the game they love within the context of an organisation that has clear and strong values about how a group of people should behave—even on the football field.

The influence the club has had on people has gone way beyond the development of their football skills. Crossway FC has been a place to find friendship and support, an environment in which characters have grown and been strengthened. When I was invited to join, it was still in its infancy. Surrounded by an engaging group of enthusiastic young men in a brand-new team, who played the game out of a sheer desire to have fun and to share their faith, my love for football returned, stronger than ever.

Our daughter, Megan, breezed into our lives and awakened a third passion in me—to accompany those I already had for my faith and football. She renewed my love of family and, along with her, God sent a calling for me: to be a father and to help others to be fathers too. My good friend Dirk Uitterdijk helped me to identify and nurture this new vocation by getting me involved in work to support the fathers in our church. He used his own extensive experience of delivering parenting courses to encourage and mentor me as his co-leader in delivering the Daddy Cool! parenting programme. My life was now changing rapidly and momentously. Megan's arrival gave Su and me an increased sense of being a family and, as a consequence, it felt as though my future direction in terms of work was becoming clearer too.

Su often brought Megan to watch me play football, which perhaps explains why Megan now has no interest in the game whatsoever! As a baby and toddler she was just happy to be out in the fresh air and running around on the grass. What was going on alongside her with all those men running and shouting was purely incidental. One morning, when Megan was two years old, Su woke up and declared that she was ready to add to our little family unit, and it was not long before she became pregnant for a second time. I could not possibly have expected that by the time our son Billy was born, my football ambitions would have been dealt a blow from which they could not ever expect to recover.

I was playing for Crossway FC in a match at well-known playing fields on Jericho Lane in Liverpool. Part way through the second half of the match I went in for a 50:50 ball and came out of the tackle with a dead leg and numbness in my thigh. It wasn't severe enough to stop me playing, but it throbbed more than a dead leg usually does. As the game progressed, my aching leg began to slow me down and I eventually started to limp, but we were into time added on and I was determined to complete the game. In the final seconds, the opposition's right winger got past our left back and was heading for the byline so, as best I could, I sprinted over and slid in to block the ball as the forward swung his leg to cross the ball. He connected with the ball at exactly the same time as me, and this time I knew my game was over. My leg was not going to carry me any further. I managed to stand while the corner was taken and then, to my great relief, the referee blew his whistle to bring the game to a close.

By the time I reached home, my leg had swollen to twice its normal size and bending it in any way was impossible. That night was the first of many sleepless ones. Every time I stood up, it felt as if my leg were a rain stick, as the pain showered from top to bottom with increasing force and intensity. When the swelling began to subside, my physiotherapist prodded and poked my leg with an increasingly quizzical look on her face. She shook her head and exclaimed how amazing it was. It did not feel amazing to me—but she was looking at it through the eyes of a collector who had come across a very rare example of her chosen object and was thrilled at her good fortune, like a stamp collector discovering a Penny Black. I had snapped one of my quadriceps, she announced—a very unusual injury in someone so young and one she had only ever come across once before in her career. She assured me that eventually, with her help, I would be able to manage sport despite my reduced quota of quadriceps, but the intense pain, the weeks off work and the resulting psychological blow made me believe that I would never play football again.

— CHAPTER 8 —

The beautiful game

I was back at work and still walking with a limp when I became the proud father of Billy. He battled for his first breath and has confronted life with purposeful resolve ever since. Despite the anguish I felt at the cruel conclusion to my football-playing days, the injury proved to be a blessing—admittedly a perspective that was only revealed by hindsight. Had I not been felled at Jericho Lane I would have persisted in playing on Saturday afternoons for as long as my legs would carry me. This course of action would have given me some short-lived satisfaction, but none of the enduring fulfilment of weekend time spent with my wife, daughter and absorbing brand-new son at the end of a week of commuting to and from my work with Customs and Excise in Liverpool.

If I had been forced to let one of my passions go, it always would have been football anyway, so stopping playing—for a second time—even though a wrench, was not the end of the world. I was fortunate to have a strong faith and a deeply loved family to compensate. I also now possessed an increasingly resolute belief that the next phase of my life should be devoted to helping other fathers. To give it my full attention, I needed to unearth an opportunity to do so in a paid capacity. I knew that, once I did, my career serving

Her Majesty in her Customs and Excise department would, without doubt or hesitation, be brought to a close. I simply could not imagine spending the next 30 years taking shelter in the stability and security of a Civil Service office, waiting to collect a substantial pension. I wanted to live for the present and reach retirement free of regrets about what could have been, so I decided to pursue my calling with vigour.

Once I had convinced myself that I should take some risks, such as accepting a lower wage, a shorter contract and less attractive pension options, and readied myself to follow God's leading, it was surprising how quickly an opportunity presented itself.

It was Dirk who had first encouraged me to get involved in supporting fathers, and he also gave me my first opportunity to devote more time to this endeavour by offering me the chance to work for him. He was employed by YMCA England—the umbrella body for the English network of local YMCAs—as their parenting development adviser, and he invited me to apply for the part-time position of 'dads and lads' development worker within his team. When I succeeded in securing the job, and HM Customs and Excise graciously agreed to my reducing my working hours to accommodate my new role, it was clear that continuing to work for the government in any capacity would be only a temporary arrangement. Not long passed before I walked away from my Civil Service office for the last time to take up part-time employment with my church, working to support fathers in the community—the perfect accompaniment to my YMCA role.

I seemed destined not to stay away from football for

long because Dirk—and the previous incumbent of my privileged position within YMCA England, Andy Howie— both understood that football was a powerful medium that could be used to deepen relationships between fathers, male carers and their sons. Many of the YMCA dads and lads groups we helped to set up and support used football to engage with the families in their communities.

At this time, Dirk introduced me to a Bible verse that motivated him and which also became my inspiration: 'He will turn the hearts of the fathers to their children, and the hearts of the children to their fathers' (Malachi 4:6, NIV 1984). This became my purpose and mission. One of the ways in which I sought to fulfil this was through a project that Su and I, with the support of others in our church, initiated to reach out to the families in our community of Hoole. We could not have anticipated that these Saturday morning sessions for dads, male carers and their young children—called Who Let The Dads Out?—would later be replicated in churches throughout the United Kingdom and overseas. However, it did quickly become clear that the formula of giving fathers and their children the opportunity to spend time together with other fathers and children in a welcoming and loving environment, with cups of tea and bacon butties in abundance, worked and was needed, desired and appreciated in Hoole. The sessions became a regular fixture in the church's calendar of events.

When I look back on the life I have lived so far, I can see that there are people whose ideas and actions have influenced the direction I have taken, although at the time I was unaware of the significance of what they had done, and so were they. One of these people was Dave Brown. Dave and his sons came to Who Let The Dads Out? when it first started and attended consistently from then on. When he made the simple suggestion that the men at Who Let The Dads Out? should play football together on Wednesday nights, neither he nor I could have anticipated where it would lead.

A considerable amount of time had passed since my injury, and memories of the physical and mental agony had faded, so I accepted his invitation to play. To my surprise, I felt no pain in my leg; my three remaining quadriceps held out just fine. An even greater surprise was how strongly my feelings for the game came flooding back.

To be honest, I have often wrestled with the phrase 'the beautiful game' and whether football really lives up to it. I think the game often just creates an illusion of beauty. At times the fluid movement of the ball and the synchronicity of the players combine to give it an elegant and graceful appearance, and the qualities of cooperation and self-sacrifice evident in a successful team are certainly beautiful attributes. But surely the evocative term 'beautiful' cannot accurately describe a whole sport, when that sport is sometimes characterised by greed, petulance and even violence? The context in which the word 'beautiful' is more commonly employed—to describe an attractive woman— seems so much more appropriate.

But perhaps we use the word 'beautiful' too cheaply when describing both football and women. Occasionally I have met women who at first glance seemed beautiful, only to find that impression rapidly dissolve when they began to speak—appearances betrayed by, for example, a tendency to coldness, snobbery or even nastiness. The skin-deep beauty was not backed up by what lay beneath, and very quickly the woman's looks began to seem less than perfect too.

What makes a woman entitled to the label 'beautiful', for me, is her soul. In other words, her thoughts, her feelings, her character—the essence of her. It is these things that define a woman's beauty, and the evidence of them can be seen in her eyes, her smile, her words and her actions. Beautiful looks make an immediate impact. A beautiful soul leaves an enduring imprint.

The same is true of football. Injury, unfulfilled dreams and even death had left me disenchanted with the sport. To feel truly at ease with describing it as a beautiful game I needed to discover its soul, or it would once again become just a temporary lover with whom my days were numbered. Fortunately, Wednesday night football came along and, after three decades of an on–off affair with the game, I knew I had, at last, found its soul.

Nearly all of the men who play Wednesday-night football are over 30 years old. Very few have played any sort of football since they were at school. Consequently, the standard of play is—how can I put this kindly?—mixed! Some of us struggle to make a decent pass over three yards. There is widespread misunderstanding of some rules; the way throw-ins are taken would break the heart of a referee! Often the sides are unequal because an odd number has turned up, and if anyone were to arrive with an expectation of a team structure they would quickly find themselves disappointed. However, we do have a strategy—the only one needed—and it is, very simply, to get the ball in the back of the opposing team's net.

What really defines the soul of Wednesday-night football, though, is the values by which we play. All comers are welcome; no one is ever excluded for lack of ability. We tolerate one another's weaknesses and ignore mistakes, recognising that nobody ever intends to give the ball away. We give encouragement where encouragement is needed and remain silent when we feel frustrated. We laugh a lot and count our blessings that we still have the opportunity to play football every week. The pace of the game slows year on year, but we play on with gratitude, with hope and with smiles on our faces.

On first assessment Wednesday-night football doesn't look attractive, but it is like a woman whose looks make little immediate impression: when you delve a little deeper and get to know and understand her soul, surprisingly she begins to look much more beautiful. In fact, you can easily find yourself falling in love with such a woman, despite your initial reluctance, and you soon realise that she is worth hanging on to. When I discovered Wednesday-night football, my zeal for the game flourished with greater intensity than ever before. It was indeed like meeting an old friend and through more mature eyes realising how beautiful she is and then falling head over heels in love with her. I look forward to Wednesday night more than any other evening in the week because it is a gathering in which I feel I belong, I have fun and I stay fit. There is no better place for me to express my love for what I have eventually discovered is truly 'the beautiful game'.

Along with thousands upon thousands of other men and boys, I was never able to fulfil my dream of becoming a professional footballer, but I have realised that it is unlikely that being paid to play the game would have brought me anywhere near as much satisfaction as I get from a kickabout with my friends on a Wednesday night. It is about as far removed from top-flight football as it is possible to get, but I have discovered that the soul of the game is not in high achievement or astronomical wages or universal adulation but in finding the right people to play the game with. The same is true of life. If you form the right relationships, you find the soul of what it means to exist and you are more likely to feel the contentment and fulfilment we all crave.

I count myself blessed indeed, because I have a relationship with God who gives me purpose and is my guide, I have a family I cherish and who love me, I have loyal and dependable friends, and, of course, I have—every week—Wednesday-night football.

PART 2

Soccer soul

*All that I know most surely about morality
and the obligations of man, I owe to football.*

ALBERT CAMUS (1913–60),
FRENCH PHILOSOPHER, NOVELIST AND GOALKEEPER

The following pages move from life story to a series of reflections on life and the Christian faith, which take football as their starting point. These can be dipped into and out of as wished.

Dedicated followers of football

It is little wonder that people liken football to a religion. The sport can obsess and consume a person to such an extent that his or her life would be more or less empty if football were to disappear overnight. Family commitments are organised around fixtures; household budgets can be decided upon only once season-ticket fees have been subtracted; and even the colours of cars, clothes and décor are influenced by the kits of supported—and unsupported—teams.

Football not only dominates the lives of individuals, it can also monopolise whole communities. On the streets of many cities football is the first, last and only topic of conversation when people meet, whether they be friends or strangers. The mood of a society—even a nation—can be altered by the result of a football match. All sorts of outrageous views and behaviour are justified by the unanimous love for a particular team.

So let's take a look at the similarities between football and religion and try to reach some conclusions about whether football is really a religion.

Firstly, in a religion there must be a deity—a god: someone or something to follow and worship. Football certainly has that; the teams we support are gods to many. They can do no wrong and they inspire unswerving loyalty, with people willing to sacrifice friendships, family relationships and economic stability for the love of their team.

A religion has followers, whose faith defines their identity. Like religious zealots, football supporters wear belief in their teams with pride. They tattoo the club name on to their skin, display the crest in car and house windows and dress in team colours. I even once saw that an especially intense devotee had incorporated the initials of his football team into the wall of his house with contrasting coloured bricks. He might be called an extremist.

A religion has a code to live by, a set of principles. The football fan's code includes tenets such as: to be a real fan you must go to watch all the matches; you must never say anything positive about another team, particularly one's closest rivals; if you go to watch an away match you must stand, not sit, throughout the game; and you must confess that the referee is always biased against us, never for us (in other words, the decisions made in our favour are correct; those made against us are mistakes). There are many others, and, as with religious believers, football supporters will vary in their views of what a fan's ethics should be and how closely they follow those ethics.

A religion has a gathering of followers for worship, and so does football. Fans gather at their churches, or grounds as they are more commonly called, and together express their love for their team. People sing, shout, wave flags and sometimes even weep in a public display of loyalty and adoration.

A religion offers hope—not just a general yearning, but a specific expectation of life after death—whereas football holds out nothing beyond the grave. It is now that we begin to realise that football is not a religion; it is just not profound or important enough. Football is simply a pastime—a diversion from the serious subjects of life and death. Bill Shankly said, 'Some people believe football is a matter of life and death. I am very disappointed with that attitude. I can assure you it is much, much more important than that.' For once, I disagree with him. Football should not be solemn; that is not its purpose. Football is for enjoyment. It allows us to escape earnestness and gives us temporary shelter from our ordered lives. Religion, on the other hand, is serious because it does concern matters of life and death.

I believe that we place football in entirely the wrong realm when we liken it to a religion. We misappropriate it, and this leads to our misusing it; we then miss out on all the good things football has to offer.

A story I love, which illustrates my point perfectly, is the Christmas Day truce of 1914, in which German and British soldiers temporarily stopped killing each other, climbed out of their trenches and had a kickabout with a football. It is a heart-warming tale and demonstrates just how powerful and positive football can be. However, we must also acknowledge that it wasn't the game of football that stopped the troops fighting; it was the religious festival of Christmas and all it stood for that made them lay down their arms. But, once they had done that, what better way to pass the time than a game of football? I can imagine them smiling, laughing, applauding each other and shaking hands.

Christmas was serious. It *was* a celebration, but a celebration of a momentous event—the birth of Jesus—that would give hope and life, and it caused a time of peace in the midst of a battle. The impromptu kickabout wasn't serious; it was a cheering and refreshing diversion. And we must never diminish the sport by making more of it than that, otherwise we miss out on its true magic, which is that, when all is said and done, football is, and always should be, fun.

That is not to say, however, that we have nothing to learn from football. The quote from the French writer and philosopher Albert Camus at the beginning of this section suggests that the language, principles and experience of football can teach us much about what it means to be human. During the 2011/12 football season I began to reflect on football stories, incidents and issues and how they might be used to shed light on passages in the Bible. I wrote my musings into a series of articles called 'Soccer Soul'. It was an enjoyable way of interpreting tricky concepts and I found that my understanding of some biblical principles was deepened by using football allegories.

I hope that using a fun pastime to illuminate matters of life and death does not risk diminishing the seriousness of those issues. My intention is the opposite, and I take encouragement from the fact that the man I follow, Jesus, often used stories that were culturally relevant to his listeners to explain his messages. In following his example I hope that my words help to reveal the truths he shared.

✚

A new season

I've experienced 40 starts to football seasons in my life so far, and the thrill I feel has never diminished. I still look forward to the first day of the new campaign with expectation and excitement. If I'm honest, the period of the year I enjoy least is from June to August. This is partly because—and you may find this strange—I dislike the long days and warm weather, but I can also attribute some of my summer gloom to the fact that no football is played. However, despite my undiminished appetite for this wonderful sport, I could never advocate a continual football season. I recognise that a spell of absence—and the old adage is right here—does indeed make the heart grow fonder. If it wasn't for the summer vacation, perhaps my enthusiasm would begin to wane and I wouldn't appreciate the start of the new season quite as much. I do love fresh starts: they energise, revitalise and liberate me.

You may have heard the phrase 'born again' in the context of the Christian faith and wondered what it means and where it comes from. Put very simply, 'born again' is another way of describing a fresh start. Jesus used the phrase in conversation with a religious leader called Nicodemus, when explaining how somebody could join God's kingdom (John 3:1–21). In essence, Jesus was saying that a person needed to decide to make a fresh start. This means committing the future to God and following Jesus

Christ's teaching; in other words, becoming a Christian—a follower of Christ.

It is a fresh start that Jesus promises will energise, revitalise and liberate, and the effects will not wear off quite as quickly as the impact of a new football season! 'For God so loved the world that he gave his one and only Son, that whoever believes in him shall not perish but have eternal life' (John 3:16).

Understanding the coach

Put yourself in a child's football boots. We coaches must be difficult to understand at times. What possible reason could there be for asking them to stand on the spot and stretch their muscles, for making them repeat the same movement over and over again during a drill and for getting them to kick the ball with the foot they wouldn't naturally use? Their young minds simply cannot comprehend why these things are so important to the enjoyment and satisfaction they will get from the game in the long term. It is understandable that sometimes they get frustrated and whine, 'Can we play a match now?'

From time to time I find myself feeling the same way about God. Why must I forgive when I do not want to? Why must I remain faithful when there is so much temptation and no one has to know? Why must I love my neighbour and, worse than that, love my enemies too?

In his book *I Was Just Wondering* (Eerdmans, 1998), the writer Philip Yancey explains that he has an aquarium in his study, and he reflects that looking after the fish has taught him 'a deep appreciation for what is involved in running a universe'. He concludes:

I often long for a way to communicate with those small-brained water-dwellers. Out of ignorance, they perceive me as a constant threat. I cannot convince them of my true concern. I am too large for them, my actions too incomprehensible. My acts of mercy they see as cruelty; my attempts at healing they view as destruction.

Like the fish in the aquarium, we will probably continue to misunderstand the God who runs our universe, but if we begin by accepting that his motives are good, we may find we are able to trust him a little more.

✤

Footballers' fuel

When I was a lad playing junior football, our half-time snack was always a quarter of an orange, carefully prepared by the mother of one of the boys. None of us was ever actually hungry halfway through a match, but sucking all the juice out of an orange seemed the right thing for a footballer to do. We were sure that our professional playing heroes did the same. As I got older and played football at clubs with better facilities, the quarter orange was replaced by a very civilised half-time cup of tea and a biscuit.

Not surprisingly, things have changed a little now. I am told that the half-time fare on the tables in Premiership changing rooms consists of Jaffa Cakes and Jelly Babies. But why? Are these the only snacks that will satisfy the babyish taste buds of the seemingly ever-younger football players? No. There is no doubt that Jaffa Cakes and Jelly Babies taste great, but they also offer more. They are low in fat and high in energy. Fat is a hindrance to a sportsman or -woman, but energy helps them to play better. So footballers don't eat such treats just for their flavours; they eat them to maximise performance.

In Psalm 34:8 it says, 'Taste and see that the Lord is good.' If you allow yourself to test God's flavour, you may find that not only does he 'taste' good but, like a Jaffa Cake or a Jelly Baby to a footballer, he will help you to prepare for what is ahead, giving you the energy you need to face the challenges of the day. So why not sample a new taste and start the day with a prayer?

The 10,000 hour rule

There is a theory floating around the sporting world that a player must have completed 10,000 hours of practice before he or she becomes world class in their chosen field. This equates to 20 hours of training per week for ten years, so it's a fairly tough schedule to maintain.

Even if you think that this is a little extreme, there is no doubt that training does improve our skills. When we practise enough, our responses to situations become automatic because our brains recall how we have dealt with them in the past and react accordingly—often without any conscious thought. An example from a different sphere of life is how we drive cars. After many years of experience on the road we can sometimes make journeys with what feels like such little concentration that when we reach our destination we wonder how we got there! We have become conditioned to such an extent that we can cope with practically every possible occurrence.

Footballers are no different. It is often amazing to see how quickly they can receive a ball, control it, throw off a defender, turn and pass it to a teammate. If they had to think about it, they would quickly lose possession of the ball. It is largely practice that has given them this ability to do the right thing with the ball in whatever situation they encounter.

In one of his letters, the apostle Paul encourages Timothy to adopt a similar approach to life, and the training schedule he recommends involves reading the scriptures: 'All Scripture is God-breathed and is useful for teaching, rebuking, correcting and training in righteousness, so that the servant of God may be thoroughly equipped for every good work' (2 Timothy 3:16–17).

Devoting 20 hours a week to anything is a tall order, but perhaps if we spent a little more time each week reading and reflecting on the guidance for life that the Bible contains, like a footballer, we too would enhance our ability to do the right thing in whatever situation we encounter.

Unexpected call-up

Imagine that you are a 48-year-old civil servant, whose only experience of playing football is kicking a ball around with the kids in the garden and the occasional game of five-a-side with a group of mates. One day you receive a phone call and are surprised to hear the manager of the national team on the other end of the line. You are even more surprised to hear that he has selected you to play for the national team. You arrive at training and discover that the other men who have been called up include a 25-year-old who has not played since he was in his Cub Scout team and a pair of brothers who have never even owned a football. It's ridiculous, isn't it? It makes no sense. Although some of us would dearly love to play football for our country, we accept that there is no place for us in the team and entirely understand why that is.

When Jesus selected his team—the men who would be responsible for conveying his message to the world—he did not make obvious choices. He did not pick religious leaders and preachers, experts in theology and experienced communicators, to be his disciples. Instead he chose fishermen and a tax collector, people who were apparently as unsuitable for the task as a middle-aged office worker would be for representing his country at football. Clearly, Jesus had a different way of looking at people and assessing their potential.

When Samuel was sent by God to anoint the person who would become king over Israel, he was about to choose the wrong person. God said to him, 'The Lord does not look at the things people look at. People look at the outward appearance, but the Lord looks at the heart' (1 Samuel 16:7).

So don't be constrained by your own feelings of inadequacy, doubts about how you look or lack of self-confidence. There is a place for you on God's team.

Cloning Jamie Carragher

If you could clone a footballer, who would it be? Would you select a prolific goalscorer of Cristiano Ronaldo's calibre, a midfield dynamo such as Xavi, or a player with a safe pair of hands such as Pepe Reina? I would choose a player who gives 100 per cent commitment to every single game he plays in. He is a defender, a strong leader and organiser on the pitch and a great ambassador for football off the pitch. His name is Jamie Carragher.

The crowd at Anfield sometimes sing a song called 'We All Dream of a Team of Carraghers' to the tune of 'Yellow Submarine'. But if it were possible to clone Carragher, would eleven versions of him make a good team? Let me give you a clue.

Carragher has played over 670 games for Liverpool, and in that time he has only ever scored five goals. Consequently, a team of Carraghers would not concede many goals, but neither would it score many. Most of its games would end in 0–0 draws, and you cannot win leagues on 0–0 draws. So a successful team needs a mix of skills and qualities, and each person must be valued for his or her contribution to the team.

In biblical times, Paul wrote a letter of advice to a church in the Greek city of Corinth that was experiencing problems of disunity. In it, he encourages more of a team attitude: 'If the whole body were an eye, where would the sense of hearing be? If the whole body were an ear, where would the sense of smell be? But in fact God has placed the parts in the body, every one of them, just as he wanted them to be' (1 Corinthians 12:17–18).

Are you part of a team? Most of us are, whether it's a work team, a sports team, a family team or a church team. If you are in a team, recognise that each person is different, value your teammates and accept that you need their support. Enjoy the good times and endure the bad times— together, as a team.

Playing by the rules

Imagine that each day at work you are watched by thousands of people gathered around you, all making instant judgements about your decisions and then letting you know—often in abusive terms—what they think of you. More than that, though, you are filmed while you work and the pictures are beamed to millions around the world. The images of you carrying out your daily tasks are accompanied by a commentary in which your mistakes are pointed out, and at the end of each day clips of your errors are replayed several times from varying angles, while a panel of experts analyses your performance. You are often criticised but rarely complimented—and the failures of others are routinely blamed on you.

It wouldn't be much fun, would it? Welcome to the world of a professional referee!

At times, it seems that referees are universally disliked, despised even. And yet they are an essential element of the game of football. They make sure that the players follow the rules. Without those rules, there would be chaos on the football field. There would be more players on one team than another. Players would pick the ball up and run with it in their hands. Dangerous tackles would be made without fear of sanction. Before we know it the game would degenerate into farce—and everyone would give up and go home. So we need rules to ensure that the game works and that everyone enjoys it.

The same is true in life. If we follow the rules, things run more smoothly and everyone is better off. But what are the rules? A teacher of the law once asked Jesus which rule was the most important. Jesus said that the two most important ones were: 'Love the Lord your God with all your heart and with all your soul and with all your mind and with all your strength' (Mark 12:30) and 'Love your neighbour as yourself' (Mark 12:31).

These two commandments make for a better society, and they are a lot easier to understand than the offside rule!

The greatest player on the planet

Who is the greatest football player this planet has ever seen? Do you think it is Pelé? Or would your choice be Diego Maradona? Eusébio? Maybe even George Best, Stanley Matthews or Kenny Dalglish? Or does Lionel Messi eclipse them all? Like most football fans, you are probably convinced that you know the answer and would vehemently argue your case with anyone. Perhaps it is the player you grew up watching, or someone you think played the most entertaining football. You might even be influenced by how friendly a player was when you met him. We could debate the issue forever but, let's face it, there is absolutely no way of proving conclusively who the greatest player is. Our judgements will always be subjective, so really there is little point in getting drawn into the argument.

Jesus dealt wisely with a similar debate that broke out among his disciples. On a journey to Capernaum, the men argued about who was the greatest. When Jesus became aware of this, he called them to him and said, 'Anyone who wants to be first must be the very last, and the servant of all' (Mark 9:35). In other words, the greatest are those with genuine humility. Their greatness comes not from the scale of their achievements or the level of their abilities, but from the substance of their characters. Great people do not seek to elevate themselves, but prefer to exalt others.

It puts a wholly different complexion on the debate about who is the greatest. So, in any walk of life, look not for the person with the most skill, but for the person who sacrifices themselves for the glory or benefit of others—and then you will discover the greatest. Any thoughts now on the greatest footballer the world has ever seen?

Lionel Messi's mistakes

The football genius Lionel Messi rarely makes mistakes, but on occasions even he has given the ball away to the opposite team. Have you ever noticed how FC Barcelona respond when that happens? It is not just Messi who attempts to get the ball back; the whole team press the opposition hard to help Messi to recover from his mistake. They don't settle until the ball is back in their possession.

Imagine if it were different and Messi's teammates refused to forgive him, placing all the responsibility for rectifying his error on him alone. Barcelona would not be nearly as successful. They win games because they have a genuine team ethos. Part of their strength lies in how they respond together to individual mistakes.

Do you ever make mistakes? I know I do. On a football pitch I make many: I miss tackles, my shooting is wayward and I have even been known to score own goals! I also make mistakes with my family and friends: I say the wrong things, I upset people and I let people down. Clearly it is right for me to say sorry; then the thing that gives me a sense of freedom is knowing that God, my family and my friends will forgive me and help me to put things right.

In a sermon he preached, Jesus promised us God's forgiveness for our transgressions, but he also encouraged us to show the same mercy to others: 'If you forgive others for the wrongs they do to you, your Father in heaven will forgive you' (Matthew 6:14, CEV).

So let us remember to be kind and compassionate when a teammate, friend or family member makes a mistake, because a day will come when we are sure to need the same grace shown to us. Our teams and relationships will be much stronger if we follow the example set by Messi and his mates!

Footballers and greed

It is very easy to talk about footballers and greed. They seem to go together like salt and pepper or fish and chips, don't they? How can the stars of the game possibly not be greedy when they earn ridiculous amounts of money, wear expensive clothes, live in mansions and own several luxury cars each? It's certainly difficult to defend wages of £100,000 a week, but can we really conclude that all of those who earn that kind of money are greedy?

Perhaps we have a tendency to think that anyone who earns more than our own salary is greedy. However, if we were offered an astronomical pay rise, I suspect most of us would accept it. Or maybe we have in mind a figure that is an acceptable level of personal wealth; anything above it moves the person who earns it into the greed category. Our greed threshold then rises in proportion to our own wealth.

Matters of money always seem to be controversial, but what can you expect? After all, as the Bible says, it is the root of all evil. But the Bible doesn't actually say that. In Paul's first letter to Timothy he warns that 'the love of money is a root of all kinds of evil' (1 Timothy 6:10). It is not money itself that is the root of evil; it is our love of it. It is not the amount we earn or own that makes us greedy; it is our attitude to it.

I have to ask myself some challenging questions to find out whether I am greedy:

- Do I have an excessive desire for wealth?
- Am I constantly eager to make more money or own more things?
- Is the level of money on offer the most influential factor when I make career decisions?
- When I am choosing how to spend it, does my desire to save money overwhelm all other considerations?

Regardless of the level of my bank balance, it is only when I can answer 'no' to all of these questions that I can truly conclude I am free from the restricting consequences of the love of money.

The language of football

If you watch a lot of football on television, you will know that the close-ups often reveal less than wholesome behaviour being displayed and offensive language being used by players and spectators. Players lose their temper, shouting and swearing at the opposition and officials. The fans chant obscenities and sing slanderous songs. It can make watching football an uncomfortable experience and an inappropriate one for the young and impressionable. Delicate ears and sensitive souls often need protecting from the untamed tongues of others.

In his letter to the tribes of Israel, James describes the tongue as a fire that cannot be tamed. He says that, for such a small part of the body, the tongue can be an incredibly powerful force: 'Consider what a great forest is set on fire by a small spark' (James 3:5). He adds that the tongue can be a powerful force for evil as well as for good:

'With the tongue we praise our Lord and Father, and with it we curse human beings, who have been made in God's likeness. Out of the same mouth come praise and cursing. My brothers and sisters, this should not be' (James 3:9–10).

The language of football or any other walk of life does not need to be foul and abusive, so although the tongue is difficult to train, we must never give up trying.

Giving it 100 per cent

Have you ever played football with a teammate who decided not to put their maximum effort into the game because they were not in the right frame of mind for it? More than likely, you will have responded with frustration and annoyance rather than attempting to understand the reasons for your fellow player's apathy. But is lack of effort ever justified?

Sometimes a half-hearted performance occurs simply because a player cannot be bothered; they are just not in the mood. Other shortages of endeavour have been protests against managers who have made unpopular decisions. Is failing to try a legitimate way to register a complaint? What about the impact on fellow players and fans? Many rise above their feelings by focusing on the fact that they are not just playing for themselves or their unreasonable managers, but for greater causes such as the team's achievement and the entertainment of supporters.

Most of us struggle for motivation at one time or another—maybe in our jobs or families. Perhaps we could all benefit from remembering that we are working for a greater purpose. In the letter Paul wrote to the Christians in Colossae, he encouraged them to remember who they were serving: 'Whatever you do, work at it with all your heart, as working for the Lord, not for human masters... It is the Lord Christ you are serving' (Colossians 3:23–24).

When we accept that we are working for God, it is certainly difficult to argue with the principle of giving 100 per cent effort all of the time.

The trials of a football fan

Most football fans know what it feels like to go through tough times. In the overall scheme of things, a run of losses or a spate of injuries experienced by our favourite team is not really that serious, but it can be a little disheartening. For some, the trials and tribulations of supporting a team become overwhelming and lead them to give up watching football. They then seek Saturday-afternoon entertainment elsewhere—even resorting to shopping trips to fill the void left by their disillusionment with the game!

Occasionally, however, we can take great encouragement from seeing a group of fans who seem to relish their team's constant struggles, whose enjoyment comes from the continual battle for their few and small successes. Their perseverance is admirable, and their achievements are sweeter because they are so hard won.

In James's letter, he encourages the early Christians to adopt a similar attitude to life. 'Consider it pure joy, my brothers and sisters, whenever you face trials of many kinds, because you know that the testing of your faith produces perseverance' (James 1:2–3).

Let's face it, it is very difficult to approach setbacks with 'pure joy', but we must also be honest and say that we often do learn from our struggles, and our characters become stronger as a result. Perhaps the greatest outcome is, as James concludes, that we develop perseverance. In other words, we master the skill of never giving up—which is always a handy quality to have!

It's all Wayne Rooney's fault

Wayne Rooney and his fellow footballers have, over the years, been blamed for many of society's ills and derided for their lack of restraint and seemingly invisible moral boundaries. What a poor example they set for the younger generation, we say.

But are we right? Should we expect sportspeople to be role models for our children? Very few would say that it does not matter how footballers behave, but it could be argued that we are guilty of over-emphasising the influence some sportspeople's misconduct has on our young people—perhaps as a way of avoiding facing up fully to our own responsibilities to set an example.

The biggest influencers of our children are the people they have direct relationships with: parents, grandparents, godparents, uncles, aunts, youth leaders, teachers and sports coaches. It is we who are most able to impart principles and values to our children and, most importantly, to teach them a sense of right and wrong. It is our responsibility to be good role models in all things and at all times, because our children are copying us. If we swear and shout when something angers us, our young ones are highly likely to grow up doing the same. If we cannot enjoy socialising without getting drunk, they will follow our example. If we gossip about and criticise our friends, their tongues will be equally loose.

So the responsibility is ours, and we must not transfer it on to some well-known but distant footballer. In his Sermon on the Mount, Jesus spoke to the crowd about the human tendency to do this, saying:

Why do you look at the speck of sawdust in your brother's eye and pay no attention to the plank in your own eye? How can you say to your brother, 'Let me take the speck out of your eye,' when all the time there is a plank in your own eye? You hypocrite, first take the plank out of your own eye, and then you will see clearly to remove the speck from your brother's eye.
MATTHEW 7:3–5

In essence, Jesus was saying that before we criticise others for their behaviour, we should first address the deficiencies in our own characters. Before we blame footballers, other famous people or anyone else for our children's actions, we must examine ourselves and address any less than desirable traits that we might otherwise pass on to the next generation. In other words, we must identify and deal with the 'plank' in our own eye before we attribute the world's ills to the speck in Wayne Rooney's eye.